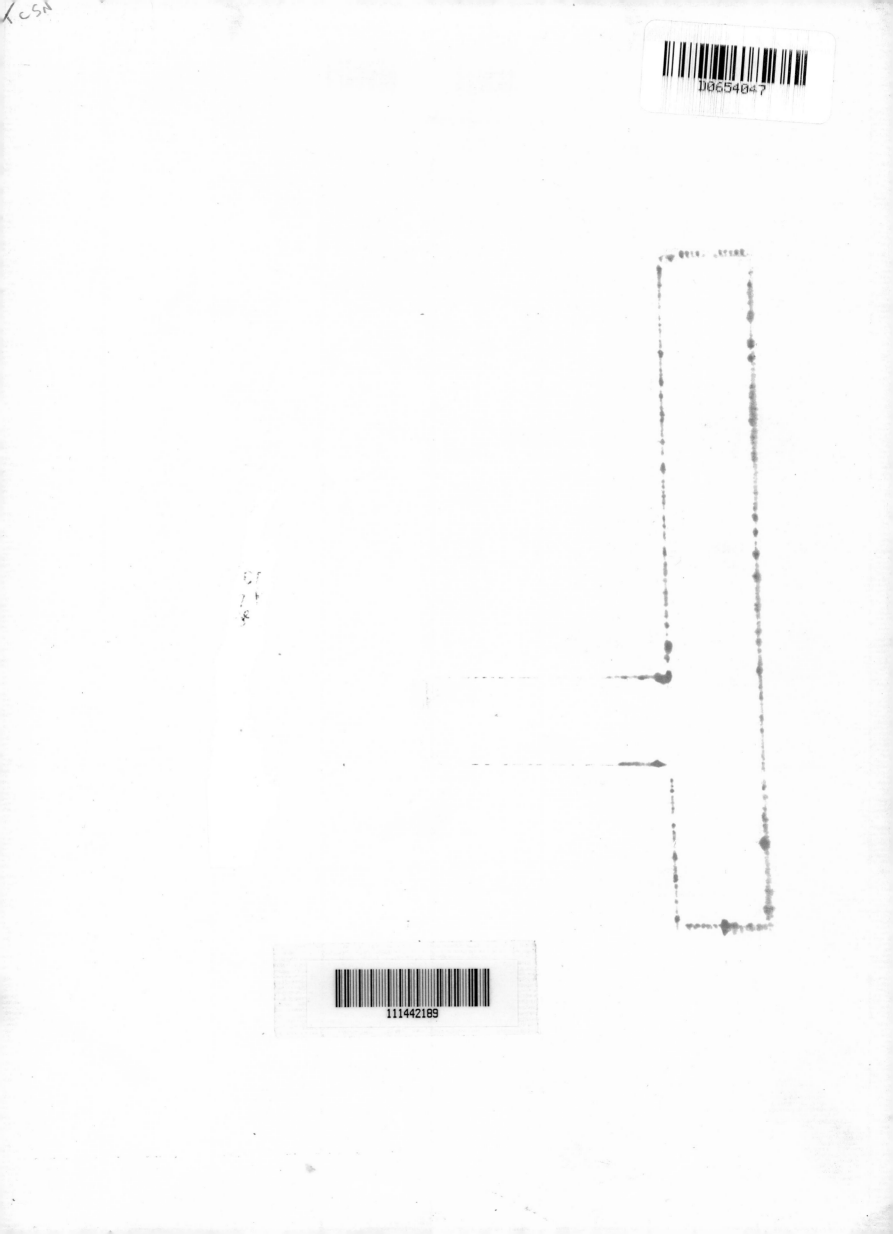

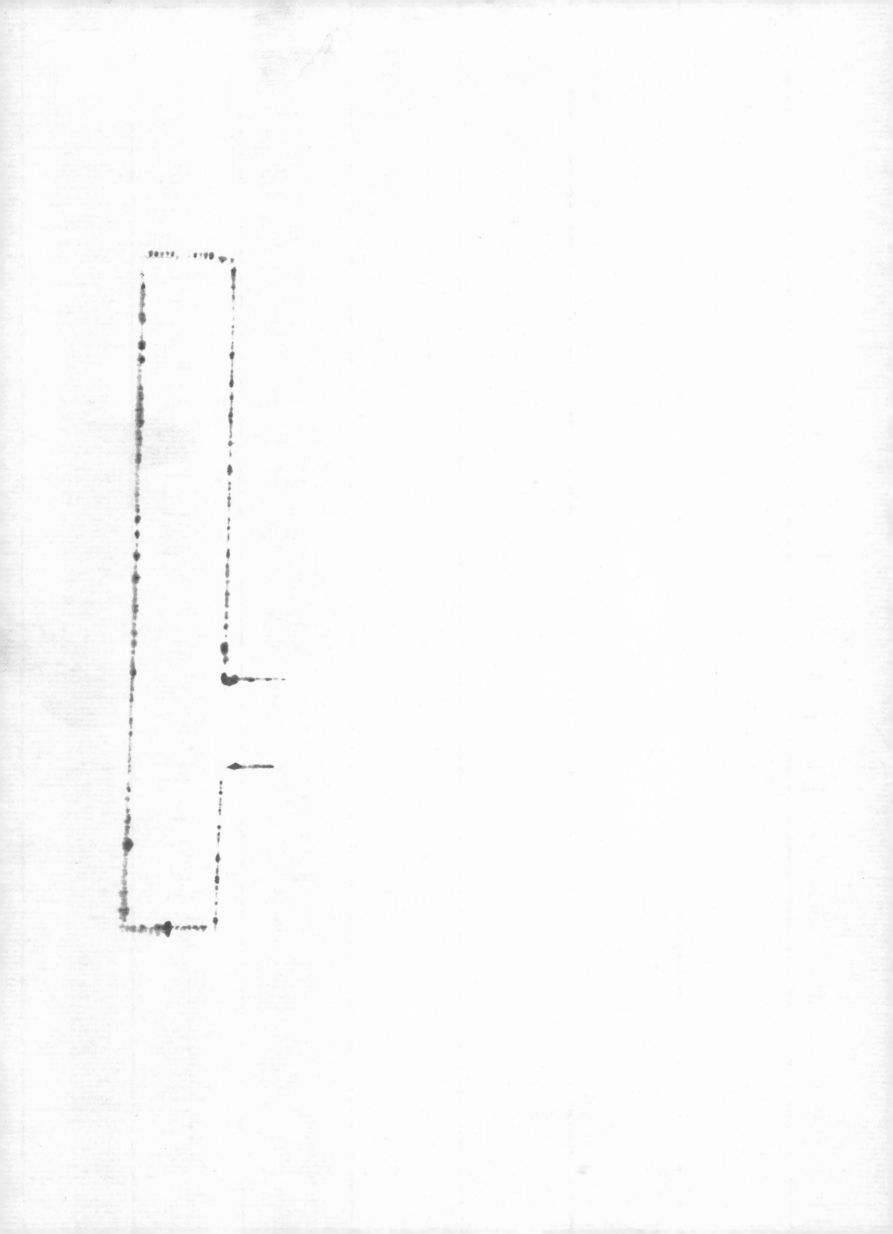

KLIMT-SCHIELE-KOKOSCHKA

HANS PLANK

KLIMT-SCHIELE-KOKOSCHKA
THREE EXPRESSIONISTS AND THEIR SUCCESSORS

ZACHARY KWINTNER BOOKS LTD.

Translated by Stephen Gorman

© 1991 by Berghaus Verlag D-8347 Kirchdorf/Inn
This 1991 Edition published by
Zachary Kwintner Books Ltd.
6/7 Warren Mews, London W1P 5DJ
ISBN 1 872532 42 X
Printed in Germany − Imprimé en Allemagne

CONTENTS

INTRODUCTION BY HANS PLANK   7

ILLUSTRATIONS:

GUSTAV KLIMT   15

EGON SCHIELE   31

OSKAR KOKOSCHKA   51

THE FURTHER DEVELOPMENT
OF AUSTRIAN EXPRESSIONISM   67

BIOGRAPHICAL NOTES   101

LIST OF ILLUSTRATIONS   109

"I don't believe what I see. I only believe what I do not see and what I feel." This statement from Georges Rouault points to an essential foundation of Expressionist art. It can be seen from this that what Rouault felt was a stronger reality for him than the visual. He experienced and sensed a reality which filled him with sadness and sorrow. "I am the silent friend of those who suffer in the desolate regions." His drawing thickened to stained-glass like, wide, black contours from which phlegmatic darkly glowing colours shine in anticipation of his experience of reality. Rouault experienced a miserable world, a world to pity and therefore his painting is "from the most wretched dialects, vulgar and sometimes subtle". Earliest childhood memories of illness and mental anxiety and the tension between the sexes were decisive for the work by the Norwegian Munch. Munch painted pictures like "Fear". "The Shriek", "Melancholia" which gave an immediate expression to the menace, the desire. Munch's paintings were immediately understood in Germany — especially by the painters from "Die Brücke" — their message was accepted. The "Brücke" painters Kirchner, Schmidt-Rottluff, Nolde and Heckel reacted to a world in turmoil shortly after the turn of the century with very exaggerated formulation and with a strong poster-like use of colour. This type of painting, the direct unbroken expression of vehement feelings, had a liberating and stimulating effect on artists in other countries. Heimo Kuchling wrote, "The act of van Gogh, Munch and the actual Expressionist to have changed 'world interior' (Rilke) into a picture world, to have given form to fears, aggression, compulsions and outbursts of constraint became an act of establishment." It was this act of establishment which also influenced art in other countries.

In Austrian painting around the turn of the century, realistic and historicizing tendencies and the sumptuous decorative style of Makart still continued to be felt. At the beginning of his career, Vienna's leading painter Gustav Klimt was still under this effect when he was entrusted with large commissioned works in the late 19th century decorative style of painting. In his youth Klimt worked as Makart's assistant. To a certain degree the climbing plants of Art Nouveau which considerably loaded Klimt's painting for many years can be seen as a further development of Makart's artistic flamboyance. Gustav Klimt's artistic path formed the bridge — not just chronological — in Austrian painting between the 19th and 20th centuries. This path which Klimt took led from the decorative representational style of art through his Art Nouveau paintings full of ornamentation to his Impressionist influenced, colourfully blossoming late work. The young Egon Schiele and for a short time also Oskar Kokoschka found their beginnings in Klimt's art. The name Gustav Klimt conjures up images of Art Nouveau, of snake-like twisting ornamentation, golden dresses and golden backgrounds interwoven with squares and oval forms in which fabulous flowers grow. A very artifical art, an art which seeks to envelop all life in a cloak of beauty, and if — very seldom — anything disgreeable enters this picture world, then only in the "convention of stylizing". (Werner Hoffmann) On ground which had become very narrow an aesthetic cult thrived (not just in Vienna) which pushed religion aside but did not yet allow the seething of the coming fall to be heard. Art Nouveau reached its peak in Klimt's work.

Before the turn of the century, Klimt worked on large commissions of a historical and allegorical nature (ceiling paintings in the Burgtheater and in the art history museum). His tendency to ornamentation increasingly pervaded his work from 1900 onwards, even in "Judith", 1901, and in paintings like "The Kiss", 1907/08, "Water Snakes", 1904/07, "Judith II", 1909, "Portrait of Fritza Riedler", 1906, positively overgrew it. In these pictures the naked parts of the bodies look as if they have been cut out. Klimt's ornamental style of decoration is extreme in the Beethoven frieze from 1902 and in the dining hall for the Palais Stoclet built by Josef Hoffmann for the industrialist Stoclet. After 1910, a feeling of relaxation entered his painting — probably under the influence of the Impressionists and Post-Impressionists whose paintings were exhibited in the Secession — the colour treatment of the picture area became more flowery and freer as in "Portrait of a Lady", 1917/18, "The Bride", 1917/18. His landscapes even before 1910 were not filled with ornamentation. Werner Hoffmann wrote that Klimt's landscape is "a brilliantly decorated nature dressed in everlasting beauty". Klimt's sketches are not, like his painting, loaded with ornament. In hundreds of sketches the artist drew almost exclusively female nudes and studies for portraits of women. The pleasure-loving erotic artist Klimt increased his mastery in supple, playfully suggestive descriptions of women's bodies and faces and sensitively and surely developed them to their utmost. Fritz Novotny wrote in 1943 about the enormous number of portrait, nude and movement studies. "They have a characteristic of the artistic expression of the highest standing: the nature-like matter-of-course with which reality is translated into an artistic graphic form. The most important thing in Klimt's art lies in the greatness of his drawing ability."

Klimt's stylistic effect on Schiele could soon be recognized and also the thematic affinity in many paintings, yet the strong inner difference is very obvious. Klimt used Impressionist influences in his later pictures. In Egon Schiele's paintings and especially in his sketches and preliminary drawings, his feelings and the driving force which made him work feverishly are expressed. Schiele's expressive art had cast off the Art Nouveau covering, ornamental effects were only evident in a few paintings. His colours were smouldering, flickering, mouldy, the figures were distorted with splayed fingers, the eyes wide open in the twisted heads. He painted landscapes with red horizons, with bare crippled trees, broken down and decaying things — and again and again self-portraits, with a tortured pose and expression. Overstimulated feverish eroticism forces and whips Schiele to produce the many crouching, squatting figures and the outspread girl nudes, the couples in folded poses. Schiele's drawing is sharp, angular, drawn in sharp scratches, breaking and cutting in the angles and edges of the gathered dresses and skirt folds. Brittle and sensitively drawn lines outline the gaunt bodies and faces, not flowing and clinging like Klimt's line.

He began in his early paintings around 1907/08 with toned painting. Around 1909/10, the dominating influence of Gustav Klimt was decisive, his ideas and ornamentation taken over directly: "Portrait of Hans Massmann", 1909, "Self-Portrait with Splayed Fingers", 1909, "Danae", 1909. However, Schiele's distinctive style of theme and execution was already evident in the painting "Dead Mother",

1910 (the emaciated mother's hand with veins and bony joints, the squarish head) and in "Portrait of Arthur Roessler", 1910, in the characteristic pose of the figure, as well as in "Portrait of Trude Engel", 1911. The young woman stands out from the undefinable toned background, with wide-open eyes, the head enveloped with a web of black hair, the sharp waviness of which is repeated in the rhythm of the folds in the dress and veil. A silhouette-like drawing structures the picture "Cardinal and Nun", 1912. The black-green background is divided into a triangular form through the abrupt red of the cardinal's cloak and hat which is cut into by the black line of the nun's costume. The contour of the nun's costume again corresponds in a parallel fashion with the sloping, hanging black curtain in the top left hand corner. On the whole, Schiele's composition was determined to a high degree by his drawing: "Portrait of Albert Paris Gütersloh", 1918, "The Family", 1918. A late autumn atmosphere, like a transition of the material world in a state of decomposition, interweaves Schiele's pictures. Schiele's early death at just twenty-eight years old in the influenza epidemic — his wife had died just three days before him with their unborn child — ended his creative activity which seems to have been complete in its clearness anyway.

The paintings of Richard Gerstl (1883—1908) seemed for the Austrian art of his time like a wild man breaking into a refined house. Otto Breicha wrote, "The primary, abrupt, direct, originality on command was his desire. Gerstl's painting was self-fulfilling in the powerful act of painting itself."

Gerstl, who was able to see pictures from the Impressionists and Post-Impressionists in the Secession exhibition of 1903 and in 1904 pictures by Munch and Hodler, had impulsively taken up the new light and colour painting style and accelerated the process in his own manner to expressive concentration and eruption. Portraits of "Alexander von Zemlinsky", "Ernst Diez", "The Fey Sisters" and landscapes, "Tree in a Country Garden". "Lakeside with Trees", have a moving spontaneous character in the exciting rhythm of their brushstroke. The most liberated and most powerful discharge of Gerstl's expressive artistic potency manifests itself in two group portraits of the Schoenberg family. Everything is centred around colour, contours only exist where colours come together and sometimes overlap each other. In a rapidly carried out piece of work, a stormy temperament captures the group of four people in a powerful colour experience of green, yellow, white, blue-black and violet tones. The representation of objects is reduced to a minimum which enables an almost unrestrained display of colour. The artist committed suicide when he was just twenty-five years old. His work burns like a solitary beacon.

After the turn of the century, art in Vienna was benetted by the decorative veil of Art Nouveau ornamentation. Oskar Kokoschka, born in 1886, quickly freed himself from this entanglement whose artistic magic dwindled away before his permeating view. The aware artist with his hard-working temperament dissected the visions, his view could no longer be blocked by empty facades. Kokoschka became one of the greatest portrait painters because his "scent" captured the psychological part of the sitter, he said that he "smelled" his models. As early as 1909 he painted such forceful portraits as "Adolf Loos", "Marquis de

Montesquieu'' and ''Marquise de Montesquieu'' in 1909/10. Around 1910 he painted the portrait of the Swiss doctor ''Auguste Forel'' where the face and hands of the figure stand out as if coming out of a veil. The ''Portrait of Baron von Dirsztay'', 1911, looks as if it was painted with hammer blows, the composition of arms and torso gives the impression that the artist would have liked to chop out the figure with an axe. Kokoschka painted transparently and thickly, he scratched contours into the wet paint with the paintbrush or with his finger nails, just as he thought suitable for the painting at hand. Apart from such portraits he also painted the picture ''Dent du Midi'', also around 1909, which is a great visionary representation of a mountain landscape in a yellow, fading winter sun. Less visionary but just as outstanding, painted thickly in compact immediacy, is the landscape from 1913 ''The Croci''. Kokoschka's artistic action had become powerful and firm, he whipped the colour in roads and streams or let it run free and stain-like. A major work, ''The Gale'', was created in 1914. This is a picture of a couple in a boat drifting in a black ocean, raised high by powerful waves; the man, Kokoschka, looks into the distance, wide awake, while the woman — Alma Mahler — sleeps by his side. The painter's power and experience create the balance in the great group painting ''The Friends'', 1917/18. This picture, one of the artist's most important, is an explosive discharge, full of winding, twisting forms and brushstrokes which jerk like bolts of lightning. The influence of van Gogh's expressive compositional rhythm had its effect in this painting.

When World War I broke out. Kokoschka signed up voluntarily. He was seriously injured on the Eastern Front and ended up in a military hospital in Dresden. He taught at the art academy there from 1919. At that time he painted the gripping picture ''Banks of the River Elbe in Dresden'' in the most powerful colours — vermillion and green — thickening block-like, probably under the influence of the ''Brücke'' artists. The ''Augustus Bridge with Steamer'' was also painted there in 1923 before Kokoschka's period of travel began. In the following years he painted numerous paintings of cities with magnificent gestures in which sometimes a Baroque conception is mixed with Impressionist highlight painting.

The humanist Kokoschka was full of sympathy for people's destitution. He wrote to Alfred Neumeyer, ''What worries me to an increasing degree is the misery of innocent children.'' In this spirit he produced the lithograph in the time of need in 1945 on which the crucified Christ has torn His hands from the Cross so that the starving, freezing children under the Cross can drink the blood form His hand.

The paintings by Albin Egger-Lienz appeared on the artistic landscape of Austria as if by brute force. Egger's painting was not essentially determined by Expressionist intention, he sought to symbolically capture human existence in its peasant form of appearance and to raise it to monumental form. In his painting there are not the strong colours of Boeckl, nor the charged atmosphere of Kokoschka, nor stirring brushstrokes as in Gerstl's paintings. Egger's frugal colourfulness is reduced to earthy tones such as brown, ochre, greenish, reddish colours sometimes contrasted with white and black. Through the simple, generously summarized drawing, through tone differences and through rather strong shadowing he gave figures and objects a sparse, emphatic, graphic form.

Egger's figures are effective because of their simple being, their calm presence is imperturbable, they have a strong inner force: his study for "Women of War". His studies and preliminary drawings for the large figural paintings are convincing because of their freedom and depth of expression, sometimes stronger than the preconceived monumentality of the final work. Often a Tyrolean farmhouse room was a background for the action in the picture as in "Peasants Eating Lunch" or "Farmer Sprinkling Holy Water" or "Pieta" or "Women of War". This work is very expressive in the extreme scarcity of brown and ochre tones, the form of the women, suggestive of wooden sculptures, in the room which is contained to the back by the angular, hard bench. His more seldom landscapes have just as much vividness because of their large peaceful form.

Impulsively and from original depths, Herbert Boeckel prepared himself, around 1920, for a mighty expressive eruption of colour. Blue, red and white with intermediate tones in the figures and the landscape in his "Group at the Edge of the Wood" gather like immense clouds. At that time Boeckl pushed colour to its thickest concentrations as in the landscape with "Eberndorf Monastery" 1922. The black-blue mountain — the thick paint furrowed by brush and spatula — is in strong contrast to the white and red dots of houses and roofs, blending strong colourfulness with compact reality. The artist was strong enough to conquer his artistic problems in one bound and the originality and intensity of his paintings which have deep sources grasps the observer. "Bathers at Eberndorf Monastery", 1922, "A Summer Evening at Klopeinersee", "Back Rows in Berlin", 1922, can be mentioned in this context as well as "Small Family Portrait", 1926.

In his later paintings it can be seen how a development to a stronger relativity to reality took place, although the expressive impetus is not effective to the same degree. At that time, Boeckl's artistic strength — orientated on Cézanne — was directed to the representation of visible reality; he made very realistic paintings and sketches. In the last years of the war Boeckl painted the altar-wings "St. Stephen", 1943, "St. John of Nepomuk", 1943, and "Noli me tangere", 1945 in which he combined visionary angles with a relativity to reality in expressive painting.

Rudolf Wacker from Vorarlberg was a pupil of Egger-Lienz at the Weimar academy. Early in his career, he painted expressive pictures sharply accentuated in form and colour. His works have an unsparing realism and direct intensity. Around 1925, the expressive exaggeration in his painting made way for a calmer determination. He recorded his intentions in his diary, "We want to unveil things, their naked reality is mysterious enough; we want to retain the vision of the moment, to do a strict and firm type of painting, which does not provoke dreams." With this set of aims the artist became a co-founder of Magic Realism. On the other hand his sketches remained expressive to the end.

Anton Kolig was a vigorous artist of colour. Around 1912 he managed a summarizing feature of almost sketch-like looseness in his "Portrait of the Schaukal Family", with five figures, through the distribution of colour emphasis and powerful rhythmical brushstrokes. From his paintings, especially the expressive "Portrait of the Bridge with Flowers", 1913, "The Artist's Children

Taddäus and Tontschi'', 1917, and ''Seated Man in White Coat'', 1920, should be mentioned. From around 1920, the representation of the male nude became more and more a main theme for Kolig. However, in these pictures the artist adheres to an almost pure nude representation, although it is strong and colourful. He has his models take up lying, kneeling or standing poses, depending on the symbolical interpretation. From 1944 — the artist was buried and seriously injured during a bomb attack — his painting gained a visionary feature: ''Singing Choir of Women'', 1946, designs for the Festspielhaus curtain ''Pieta'' in Salzburg, 1946—49.

Josef Dobrowsky, born in Karlsbad, developed his painting most freely in the landscape paintings from around Vienna. The fields in yellow, ready to be harvested, with red stripes running through them under green or deep blue stormy skies and colourful winter landscapes with great atmospheric intensity belong to the most successful works of Dobrowsky's picturesque Expressionism.

Wilhelm Thöny's painting has a special quality. In his time in Graz the artist painted dark-coloured pictures in black and blue tones, broken by pale light tones such as in ''Banks of the Mur in Graz''. In enigmatic figural paintings, blackish figures are raised ghostlike with sharp contours, from the mysterious surroundings as in the painting ''The Bridge''. In 1931, the artist went to Paris and later to New York where he painting the atmosphere of the big city in impressive water colours.

Anton Faistauer aspired to a harmonious, refined style of painting. This inclination separated the artist from Expressionism. He was influenced by Impressionism, but sought more to consolidate the material world in his paintings and condemned an art which was nothing more than ''magic for the sensitive gourmet''. He sought ''the deeper humanity''. Sometimes the cultivated colours and the too easy-going momentum of the portrait and nude compositions were an encumbrance for Faistauer's work. As opposed to these, landscape paintings of his home in Salzburg such as ''Saalhof Castle in Maishofen'', 1916, ''Summer Snow'', 1920, ''Flower Still Life'', 1924, and portraits like ''Peasant Girl'' around 1916 and ''Lady with Hat'', 1917, as well as still lifes in dark toned harmony seem to be the most intimate among Faistauer's paintings over the years. These are the paintings which still emanate the ''sincerity'' which Faistauer sought in his paintings.

Aloys Wach, a painter from Upper Austria, went to Dresden and Paris in his younger years where he was confronted with work by the Expressionists and the Cubists respectively. In his woodcuts, etchings and sketches from that time Wach took issue with the two main art movements of the 20th century and in these prints created his most succinct work. Later in his life, Wach was too isolated and lost himself too much in speculations which had nothing to do with art and which, along with hardship at the time of the economic crisis, affected the standard and continuity of his artistic performance.

Werner Berg's work is unwieldy and contrary to all popular art styles, like an erratic block. He was equally significant as a wood carver and painter. His power of design permeated his existence in his choice home ''Lower Corinthia'' where Wach settled as a farmer on the ''Rutarhof''. There his work grew in depth and width. His work is composed of firm, clear lines which contain figures and landscape in the unmistakably characteristic work of Werner Berg. Strong emotion and spiritual clarity are combined in his paintings. The artist puts his marshalling forces against his experiences of monstrosities, picture by picture. In this way he created ground for himself in a time of distress — narrow at first, but increasing all the time — through works which matured to exemplary importance. Defying the hardship and wrongs in his difficult life, Herbert Fladerer's woodcuts developed to an inner tightness and intense statement. Fladerer's woodcuts have a unique character and are symbols of a tough, difficult and burdened existence, full of contained sincerity and still hope.

Karl Stark's pictures are a wave of colour which originated in front of the landscape, in front of the still life, in front of the human figure. The paint looks as if it has been kneaded in thick viscosity and differentiated in its values until the artist achieved a state of balance between inner form and objective appearance. Referring to Cézanne, Stark demanded a consciousness of nature. The artist's resolute artistic temperament was already evident in the sketches which he did at the beginning of the forties. Albert Paris Gütersloh wrote about Stark's numerous landscapes, "... on which the painter's brush proved its efficiency. We say brush and painter, we cannot talk about drawing" ... "Stark was concerned with the general impression."

Hans Aurenhammer, the director of the "österreichische Galerie", said, referring to Stark's straight following of his aims, "A rigorous legitimacy which left him his colour after his original experience, ignoring everything which brought and supported fashion and success, also characterised his personality."

Otto Jungwirth's work is a striking example of how an artistic work can gain inner tightness in spite of external compulsions. The humdrum of everyday life of simple city dwellers, their poverty, loneliness and sickness roused Jungwirth's compassion which also found a convincing means of expression in his drawings and paintings.

Hans Plank sought to capture experience and reality in pictures and woodcuts in a realistic Expressionism. Edvard Munch's observation, "I don't paint what I see, but what I have seen," can also be applied to the style of his creations.

This overview is certainly not complete. However, it shows how the "establishing action of the Expressionists" developed. An intrinsically valid ascertainment by Heimo Kuchling, which expresses the basic ideas behind Expressionism, also points to its continuing effect:

"Expressionism is no abstract, idealism which could lose the ground on which it was created. Expression cannot raise itself so high above the actual factors which caused it that it could lose or give up its bond to reality. Where reality attacks the artist, where it endangers or consternates him, or — in contrast — where substantial powers flow from reality and enrich him, it will force him to make an expression of his experiences. Art which is not splendid representation, which is not devotional art, which is not limited to inner artistic-formal problem posing is expressive art. The seed which Expressionism sowed sprouts in it. Changes of form are equivalent to changes of reality."

GUSTAV KLIMT

He did not see a road in front of him, much less an aim, he only felt one direction: that of his intuition. Through the middle of an unpredictable area already well furrowed with hidden paths and stumbling blocks, with even a few well-defined military roads on which other intuitive artists struggled along. They had nothing more certain than the direction. It cannot even be said forwards; the only thing that is true is that wherever they were going it was not where they all came from. Away from everything which lay behind them. The hate of the eternal over and done with united them and fraternized them. In place of the old herd a new herd. Klimt also had the strength to shake off this, to go far ahead of the rest of them in the direction in which intuition led him, his inner experience of development: Root, treetop, blossom, fruit. Now it is still blossom, what will the fruit be like? There will be no fruit. Klimt is an artist of eternal blossom, a part of the unending spring. Those are the great naive artists. They never arrive at the point. Only for them does l'art pour l'art make sense. But today's naive artist is different from yesterday's, from those from a thousand years ago. Everything that has been, has not passed him by without leaving a trace. He has had to absorb and appropriate it to himself, with or without his free will.

Ludwig Hevesi

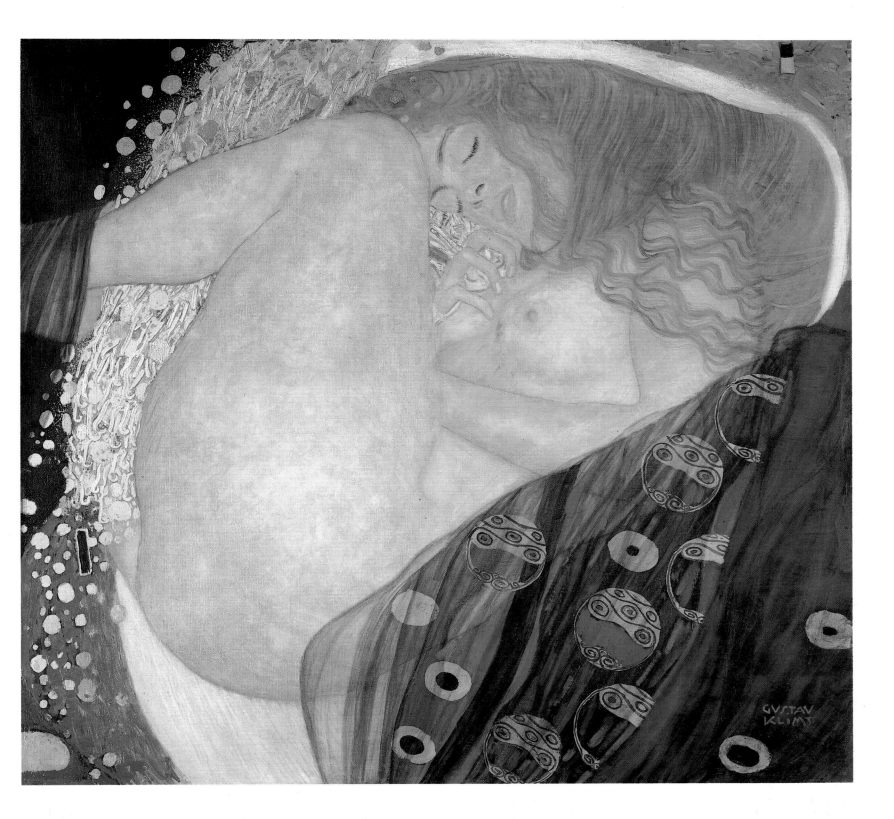

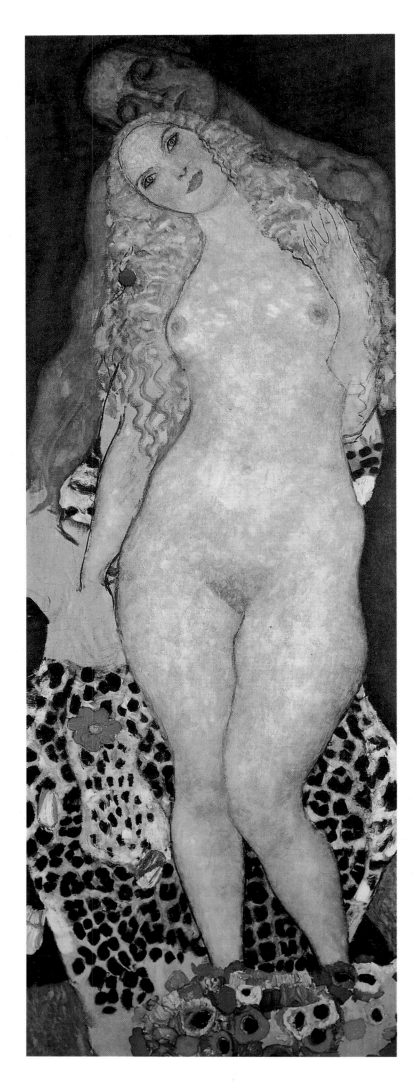

GVSTAV
KLIMT

Nachlass meines Bruders Gustav
Hermine Klimt

EGON SCHIELE

His art is monological and, in a certain sense, demono-manic. Many of his paintings are materialisations of visions which became clear in a clouded consciousness. He feels fate lurking behind his life and gives this feeling a fascinatingly obvious expression with an almost devout in-nocence. His sensitivity and receptivity to the most gentle radiations of cosmic power are astounding. Neither the mid-dle classes nor the aristocracy find their hearts, not to men-tion their souls touched by Schiele's pictures. He is outside of society, a loner. He spins wonders from his own mucilage like a spider and is set upon being an artist and only wanting to create works of art. This is why those who look for cultivated stupidity and uncultivated prejudices in any form whatsoever in his work turn away in disappointment when they do not find them. As with the old Gothic artists, Schiele's art does not arise from any great cheerfulness but from a great seriousness.

Cosmic grief is the muse of his art and its rhythm is enchant-ing.

His paintings are the strictly formal manifestations of vi-sionary, nervous sensations, sensitive impressions. His pic-tures were and are created from drive and instinct, without pretence or bitterness, completely lacking hope and there-fore they only please those who still value and do not want to miss the sensual experience of hidden, inconspicuous moments in life and their artistically executed transfer onto canvas.

Arthur Roessler

40

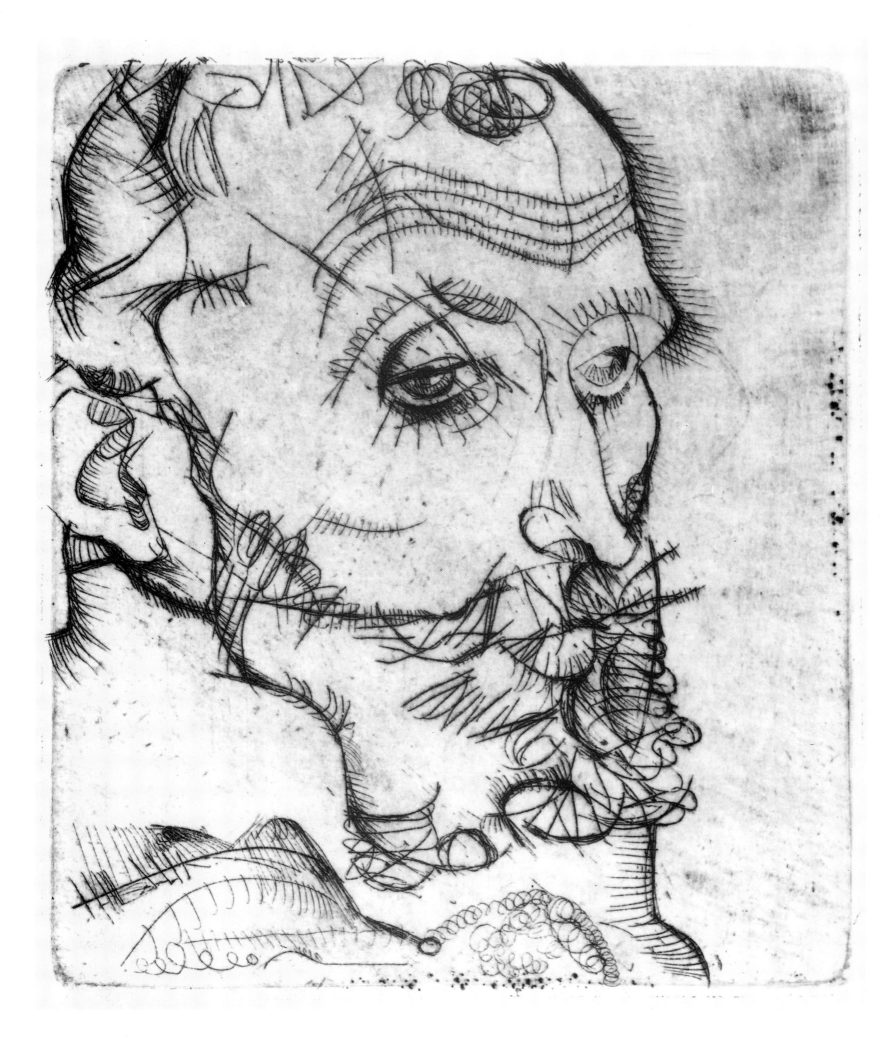

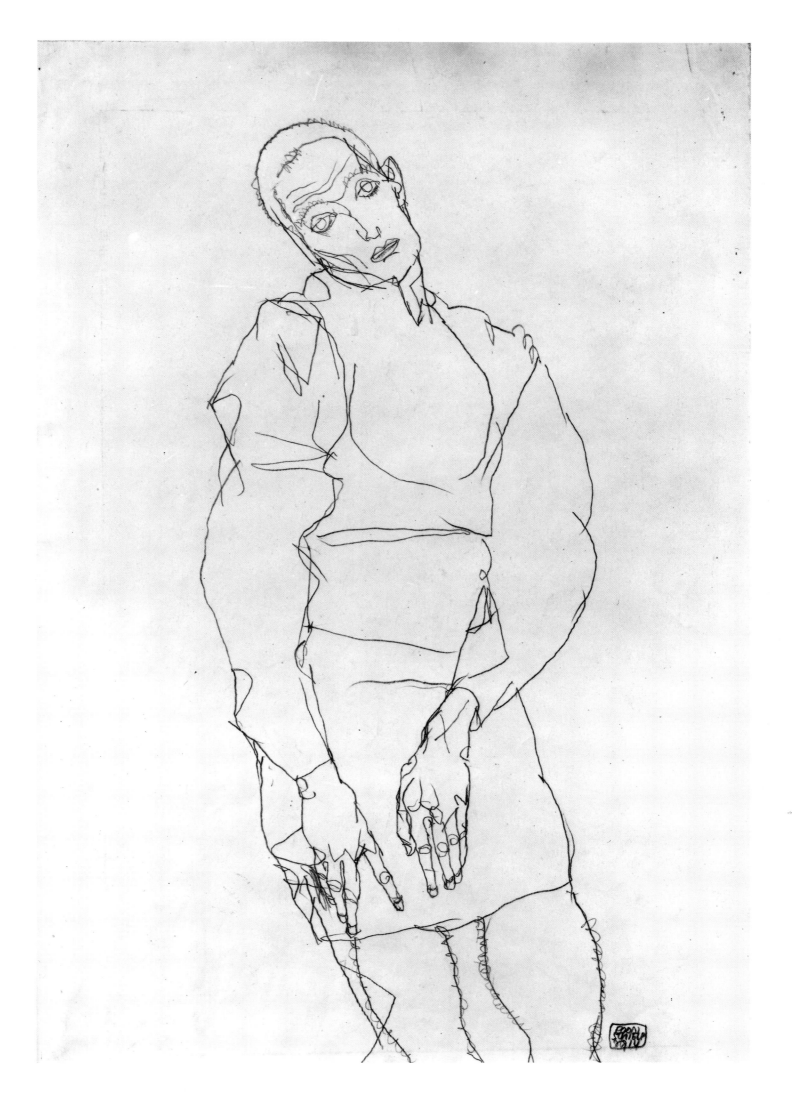

47

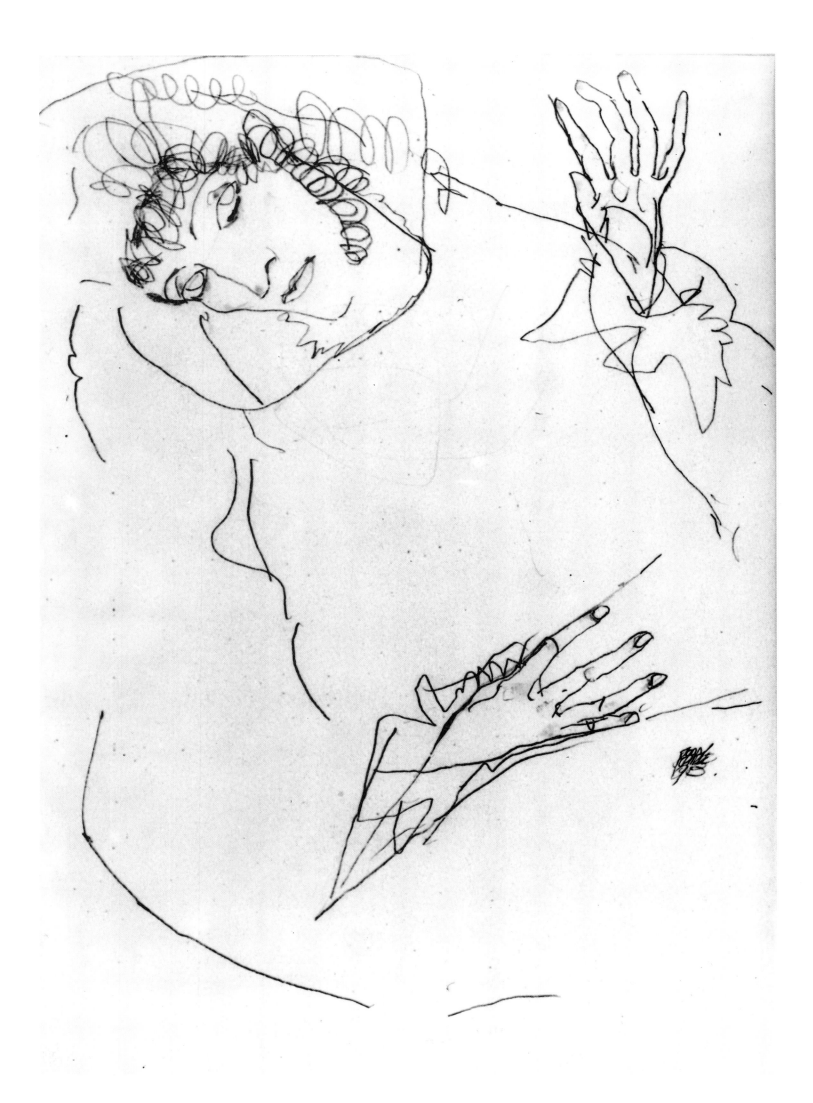

49

OSKAR KOKOSCHKA

This brilliant, stormy young man, Oskar Kokoschka's entrance to Vienna shortly after the turn of the century is unusual. His pictures caused offence and horror. They were regarded as provocative, as a slap in the face of the dominating taste. He touched on things hidden by conventions of the time. Kokoschka was not concerned with presenting the appearance of beauty, but instead with probing into the labyrinth of existence. These pictures expressed a truth, which it was forbidden to speak of in those days: life is full of anxiety and threats. These works are still disturbing today. They penetrate the skin like x-rays and expose man's substance. Adolf Loos, one of the many contemporaries who Kokoschka painted, said of his portrait, "It is more similar than me."

Later he also painted works which were created with an equal clear-sightedness. Kokoschka, in his pictures, raised what man in this century is and can be into the twilight zone. The completely unconventional and self-willed artist became the true portrait painter of our time. He wrote a more lively history of the era than many historians.

One only has to hang the paintings from a great artist on the wall to experience what has become rare in art today: real criteria. Kokoschka conquered these criteria in his pictures. He vehemently threw himself into nature and attempted to evoke it through colour. In his early period the colours are dark and overcast, then they become more robust, put on in large areas, almost gobelin-like in the Dresden period to become more lively, lighter and more festive. No-one can escape the "molto espressivo" of these pictures or their vibrant energy. They radiate a power and a fascination which sharpens and rejuvenates the senses.

Fritz Nemitz

THE FURTHER DEVELOPMENT OF AUSTRIAN EXPRESSIONISM

Whoever uses the well-known and often heard phrases: I expect of an artist, the artist should, the artist must — only proves that he does not have a clue how a work of art is created. With such demands perhaps he confronts the crafts which serve him, perhaps he raises them above the wide spectrum of artistic productions, the market ware which accommodates present needs. No person in the world has a need for the art of a genius, before it is there, apart from the person who creates it.

These days it is sneeringly asked if the artist only produces for artists. We can safely answer "Yes", but with the honorary title artist we do not just mean those who are able to "interpret" art meaning to "recreate" it. After all we live from the belief that their numbers will grow.

from VER SACRUM

80

88

97

98

99

BIOGRAPHICAL NOTES

BOECKL, HERBERT

Klagenfurt 1894 — 1966 Vienna

Herbert Boeckl originally studied architecture and, for a short time, also medicine and veterinary medicine. During World War I, when he was conscripted to do military service, he painted his first pictures. After 1920 his style became strongly Expressionistic. The wildness of his paintings at first even confused friends with an expert knowledge of art. "I hardly know another artist at present who is so far ahead of his close friends in the development of his understanding," wrote Otto Benesch.

Periods in Berlin, Paris and on Sicily, a significant influence from Cézanne's work and a profound Christian way of life all played a part in forming his work. From 1931—1965 he was a professor at the Viennese academy of art, he was also twice rector there. After the war his pictures became visionary-abstract.

He painted frescoes for the monastery Seckau/Styria which were covered for years so as not to distract the faithful. Only in recent times has it been possible for religious circles to understand his work and the deep religiousness which it contains.

DOBROWSKY, JOSEF

Karlsbad 1889 — 1964 Vienna

After his studies at the academy in Vienna and his military service in World War I, the artist turned quite early in his career to Expressionism. In 1919, just after finishing his studies, he became a member of the Vienna Secession. He was fascinated by Egon Schiele's work and also that of Anton Faistauer and Anton Kolig. His great love was the expressive landscape. Dobrowsky taught at the academy in Vienna from 1947—1963.

EGGER-LIENZ, ALBIN

Striebach near Lienz 1868 — 1926 Bozen

His origins from the Tyrolean mountains are unmistakable. His father, a church painter, allowed him to attend the academy in Munich where, at first, Defregger was his idol. The first picture which brought him recognition in Vienna was conceived completely in his spirit. But Egger soon developed his own style. His earthy, strongly expressive subdued painting began around the turn of the century. After a short period teaching at the academy in Weimar, Egger returned to his homeland, to a world which was indispensable for his work.

FAISTAUER, ANTON

St. Martin near Lofer 1887 — 1939 Vienna

Faistauer studied at the academy in Vienna (together with Anton Kolig and Egon Schiele). He was a pupil of Griepenkerl, however, he left the academy together with his friends and belonged to the "Neukunstgruppe" in 1909. He then worked in Salzburg and later in Vienna. His most important official commissions were the painting of the church in Morzg and, later, the frescoes in the Salzburg Festival House designed by Clemens Holzmeister.

FLADERER, HERBERT

Vienna 1913 —1981 Wernstein

After his training at the research and teaching institute for graphic art and at the academy for graphic art in Vienna, Fladerer was in the army until 1945. After the war he began his considerable woodcut oeuvre, worked as a graphic artist and created murals.

He was an exceptionally sensitive person; as a soldier he served on the polar front, and was faced with periods of destitution during the whole of his lifetime. With fading strength he had to work at the cost of great privation and loneliness.

GERSTL, RICHARD

Vienna 1883 — 1908 Vienna

Like his fragmentary work which is just a short burst of exceptional talent, his artistic career also shows no continuity. His attendance at the academy was interrupted several times and his completely different attitude soon forced him to leave. Even Heinrich Lefler who allowed him many special privileges could no longer retain the talented student. Gerstl gained significant impressions from Impressionism and Edvard Munch's work through the great exhibitions which took place in Vienna.

His marked musical interest led to a close contact with the Schoenberg circle. When the short friendship with Schoenberg and his wife ended, Gerstl felt isolated, as he also rejected any contact to the Secession. Klimt was, for him, a representative of the "has-beens". The hopelessness of the artistic situation led him to take his life when he was just twenty-five years old. Werner Hoffmann wrote, "He died because he had lost faith in the healing, rescuing power of the creative act."

JUNGWIRTH, OTTO

Vienna 1933 — lives in Vienna
Jungwirth studied at the academy in Vienna and received a training as teacher at the Federal College of Teaching in Vienna.
He lives as a teacher and painter in Vienna.

KLIMT, GUSTAV

Baumgarten near Vienna 1862 — 1918 Vienna
Klimt studied at the Viennese arts and crafts school and as Makart's successor he enjoyed great popularity in society with his decorative murals. As a leading Art Nouveau artist he was at first highly respected, however, his designs for the mural paintings for Vienna University caused great hostility. This ended in Klimt abandoning the commission.
Klimt's great ability had considerable influence on young artists and on Viennese artistic life. His work was the peak and at the same time the end of a great art in a forlorn world, however, it was also the germ cell, stimulus and starting point for a new disturbing lively development in our century.

KOKOSCHKA, OSKAR

Pöchlarn 1886 — 1980 Villeneuve
Kokoschka graduated from the Viennese school of arts and crafts which was in those days one of Europe's most advanced teaching institutions. He then joined the "Wiener Werkstätte" which had been founded by teachers and pupils from the school, however, he soon detached himself from their stylistic restrictions. As a painter and writer he fought against the established bourgeoisie, the performance of his play "Murder, Hope for Women" in 1909 caused a scandal —

and made him famous. The architect Adolf Loos became aware of and supported him.

Kokoschka went to Berlin where he worked for Herwarth Walden's "Sturm". An intense love affair with Alma Mahler ended dramatically after a few years. At the outbreak of World War I, Kokoschka signed up voluntarily for the cavalry. After having been seriously injured in 1915, he was brought to Vienna and then to the military hospital in Dresden. He taught at the academy in Dresden from 1919 till 1924. In the following years he travelled a lot — this is when he produced many of his famous city paintings. His ostracism in Nazi Germany forced him to spend many years in London. In 1949 he returned to Vienna. In Salzburg he founded the "School of Seeing". In 1954 he settled in Villeneuve on Lake Geneva and remained there for the rest of his life.

KOLIG, ANTON

Neutitschein in Moravia 1886 — 1950 Nötsch

After his studies at the school of arts and crafts and the academy of graphic art in Vienna, he received a grant on the recommendation of Gustav Klimt, which enabled him to spend two years in France. After his military service he settled in Nötsch in Carinthia, his wife's home. His wife was a sister of the painter Franz Wiegele. The "Nötsch School" was founded. Its main figure was Anton Kolig, but Herbert Boeckl was also closely associated with it.

In 1928 he took over a professional chair at the Stuttgart Academy until 1943, when he was finally classified as a degenerate artist by the Nazis which meant that he was not allowed to work. From 1943 until his death he lived in Nötsch where he was seriously injured during a bombing raid in 1944.

PLANK, HANS

Weng 1925 — lives in Braunau

After qualifying as a teacher, Hans Plank studied at the academy of graphic art in Vienna under Herbert Boeckl and Albert Paris Gütersloh. A study trip led him to London. He travelled to Norway, Romania, Russia and Japan.

He works as a freelance artist and woodcutter.

SCHIELE, EGON	Tulln on the Danube 1890 — 1918 Vienna

SCHIELE, EGON

Tulln on the Danube 1890 — 1918 Vienna

After his training at the academy in Vienna, Schiele's encounter with Gustav Klimt was pathbreaking for his further work. Together with his colleagues Anton Faistauer, Franz Wiegele and Albert Paris Gütersloh, he founded the "Neukunstgruppe" who had their first exhibition in 1909/10. Clearly influenced by Klimt in theme and form canon, also by Ferdinand Hodler whose works were shown in Vienna, Schiele developed very early a completely individual style and colour which make his work unmistakable. A certain animosity which he was faced with could not distract him from his path.

"Deadly threats and decline were present in this artist's work when Europe did not yet know battlegrounds..." wrote Werner Hoffmann. "He himself is, in the truest sense of the word, the focal point in which current affairs have their symbol. Schiele's life's work covers just a decade. In the beginning is the almost manic self-analysis which balances on the edge of despair, which makes way for a casual wordly view in the last years. It is as if Schiele found the hope for a new, more human human being through his marriage with Edith Harms from which his creativity received a positive attitude towards life."

Shortly before his early death an exhibition in the Secession building brought him recognition and also his first material success.

STARK, KARL

Glojach 1921 — lives in Vienna

Karl Stark received his training — interrupted by the war years which he spent as a soldier — at the master school for painting in Graz and afterwards at the academy in Vienna under Albert Paris Gütersloh and Herbert Boeckl. He has undertaken many study trips since the fifties. Apart from oil painting he has a special interest in gouache.

THÖNY, WILHELM

Graz 1888 — 1949 New York

Thöny studied at the academy in Munich under Jank and Hackl and also worked in Munich for a long time after his studies where he belonged to the co-founders of the Sezession. The outbreak of World War I put an abrupt end to the stimulating years of study. After the war Thöny returned to Graz where he was a co-founder of the Graz Secession. Thöny went to Paris in 1931. In 1938 he left Europe and moved to New York. His late works, created in America bring a completely new timbre into Expressionism.

WACH, ALOIS

Lambach 1892 — 1940 Braunau
Wach received his training by attending various art schools in Vienna and Munich. Stays in Berlin brought him into contact with the "Sturm" and Herwarth Walden, while in Munich he entered the circle around the "Blaue Reiter". A two-year stay in Paris, working at the Académie Colarossi eventually brought him to an Expressionist style. However, this had ended already by the middle of the twenties; other influences came to the forefront of Wach's work.

WACKER, RUDOLF

Bregenz 1893 — 1939 Bregenz
After his studies in Bregenz, Vienna and Weimar, where he was a pupil of Egger-Lienz, Wacker established contact with Fritz Mackensen, one of the leading artists from the Worpswede circle. As a soldier he served in Galicia and Siberia where he was taken prisoner. He could only fully develop after his return in 1924 when he at first tended towards Art Nouveau. Stays in Berlin and Vienna and a trip to Romania broadened his insight. He stayed in Bregenz from 1925, from 1925/26 he turned towards Magic Realism in his painting and became Austria's most significant representative in this style. His drawing, influenced, among others, by Kokoschka remained true to Expressionism.

LIST OF ILLUSTRATIONS

GUSTAV KLIMT
Birch Grove. 1903
Oil on canvas, 110 x 110 cm
Neue Galerie der Stadt Linz,
Wolfgang Gurlitt-Museum

17

GUSTAV KLIMT
Poppy Field. 1907
Oil on canvas, 110 x 110 cm
Österreichische Galerie, Vienna

18

GUSTAV KLIMT
Danaë. 1907/08
Oil on canvas, 77 x 83 cm
Sammlung Dichand, Vienna

19

GUSTAV KLIMT
Woman with Hat and Feather Boa. 1909
Oil on canvas, 69 x 55 cm
Österreichische Galerie, Vienna

20

GUSTAV KLIMT
The Black Feather Hat. 1910
Oil on canvas, 79 x 63 cm
Private collection

21

GUSTAV KLIMT
Avenue in the Park of Kammer Castle. 1912
Oil on canvas, 110 x 110 cm
Österreichische Galerie, Vienna

22

GUSTAV KLIMT
Portrait of Johanna Staude. 1917/18
Oil on canvas, 70 x 60 cm
Österreichische Galerie, Vienna

23

GUSTAV KLIMT
Adam and Eve. 1917/18
Oil on canvas, 173 x 60 cm
Österreichische Galerie, Vienna

24

GUSTAV KLIMT
Nude. Ca. 1907
Pencil drawing, 56.1 x 36.3 cm
Allen Memorial Art Museum, Oberlin, USA

25

GUSTAV KLIMT   26
Old Woman, Sitting. Ca. 1909
Pencil drawing with black crayon, 55 x 34.9 cm
Private collection

GUSTAV KLIMT   27
Study for the Portrait 'Adele Bloch-Bauer'. 1912
Pencil drawing, 56 x 36 cm
Galerie Würthle, Vienna

GUSTAV KLIMT   28
Girl Friends. 1913
Pencil drawing, 54.8 x 34.9 cm
Private collection

GUSTAV KLIMT   29
Girl's Head. 1913
Pen-and-ink drawing, 56.6 x 36.9 cm
Graphische Sammlung Albertina, Vienna

GUSTAV KLIMT   30
Study for the Portrait 'Johanna Staude'
Date, size and technique unknown
Whereabouts unknown

EGON SCHIELE   33
Female Nude on Coloured Blanket. 1911
Pencil, watercolours, 48 x 31 cm
Neue Galerie der Stadt Graz

EGON SCHIELE   34
Madonna. 1911
Oil on canvas, 79.5 cm x 80.3 cm
Sammlung Dichand, Vienna

EGON SCHIELE   35
Agony. 1912
Oil on canvas, 70 x 80 cm
Neue Pinakothek, Munich

EGON SCHIELE   36
Dead City. 1912
Oil on canvas, 80 x 80 cm
Kunsthaus Zurich

EGON SCHIELE   37
Portrait of Trude Engel. 1913
Oil on canvas, 100 x 100 cm
Neue Galerie der Stadt Linz,
Wolfgang Gurlitt-Museum

EGON SCHIELE   38
Nude Back of a Girl with Long Braid. 1913
Pencil, watercolours and opaque colour. 47.7 x 32 cm
Sammlung Dichand, Vienna

EGON SCHIELE   39
Self-Portrait with Red Shirt. 1914
Pencil and opaque colour on paper. 48 x 32 cm
Sammlung Dichand, Vienna

EGON SCHIELE   40
Death and Girl (Self-Portrait with Walli). 1915
Oil on canvas, 150 x 180 cm
Österreichische Galerie, Vienna

EGON SCHIELE   41
Krumau Landscape. 1916
Oil on canvas, 110 x 140.5 cm
Neue Galerie der Stadt Linz,
Wolfgang Gurlitt-Museum

EGON SCHIELE   42
Mother with Two Children. 1917
Oil on canvas, 150 x 158.7 cm
Österreichische Galerie, Vienna

EGON SCHIELE   43
Portrait of Edith Schiele, Sitting. 1917/18
Oil on canvas, 140 x 110.5 cm
Österreichische Galerie, Vienna

EGON SCHIELE   44
The Family. 1918
Oil on canvas, 149.7 x 160 cm
Österreichische Galerie, Vienna

EGON SCHIELE   45
Mother and Child. 1910
Pencil drawing, 56 x 37.3 cm
Historisches Museum der Stadt Vienna

EGON SCHIELE   46
Portrait of Franz Hauer. 1914
Dry-point engraving
Graphische Sammlung Albertina, Vienna

EGON SCHIELE   47
Male Figure, Standing (Self-Portrait). 1914
Pencil drawing, 48.2 x 31.5 cm
Nationalmuseum, Stockholm

EGON SCHIELE   48
Portrait of a Woman. 1912
Pencil drawing, 47.7 x 31.7 cm
Graphische Sammlung Albertina, Vienna

EGON SCHIELE   49
Edith. 1915
Pencil drawing, 44.5 x 30.5 cm
Graphische Sammlung Albertina, Vienna

EGON SCHIELE   50
Squatting Woman, the Left Arm Pushed Forward. 1918
Charcoal drawing, 45 x 29.5 cm
Graphische Sammlung Albertina, Vienna

OSKAR KOKOSCHKA   53
PIETA. 1908/09
Poster for the première of his drama
"Murderer, Hope of Women"

OSKAR KOKOSCHKA   54
Portrait of Herwarth Walden. 1910
Oil on canvas, 100 x 69.3 cm
Staatsgalerie, Stuttgart

OSKAR KOKOSCHKA   55
Self-Portrait with Alma Mahler. 1913
Oil on canvas, 100 x 90 cm
Museum Folkwang, Essen

OSKAR KOKOSCHKA   56
Whirlwind. 1914
Oil on canvas, 181 x 220 cm
Kunstmuseum, Basle

OSKAR KOKOSCHKA 57
Self-Portrait. 1917
Oil on canvas, 79 x 63 cm
Von der Heydt-Museum, Wuppertal

OSKAR KOKOSCHKA 58
Friends. 1917/18
Oil on canvas, 100 x 150 cm
Neue Galerie der Stadt Linz,
Wolfgang Gurlitt-Museum

OSKAR KOKOSCHKA 59
The Persian. 1923
Oil on canvas, 95 x 62 cm
Leopold-Hoesch-Museum, Düren

OSKAR KOKOSCHKA 60
Augustus Bridge in Dresden. 1923
Oil on canvas, 65 x 95 cm
Stedelijk van Abbe-Museum, Eindhoven

OSKAR KOKOSCHKA 61
Squatting Girl. 1936
Pencil drawing
Graphische Sammlung Albertina, Vienna

OSKAR KOKOSCHKA 62
Esther. 1920
Lithograph, 67 x 46 cm

OSKAR KOKOSCHKA 63
Portrait of a Gentleman (Iwar von Lücken). 1918
Lithograph, 67 x 46 cm

OSKAR KOKOSCHKA 64
Resting Woman, the Head Supported by Her Right Arm.
Ca. 1924
Chalk drawing
Graphische Sammlung Albertina, Vienna

OSKAR KOKOSCHKA 65
Study for ''Concert''
Chalk drawing
Graphische Sammlung Albertina, Vienna

OSKAR KOKOSCHKA   66
The Artist's Mother in an Armchair,
Sitting and Sleeping
Charcoal drawing
Graphische Sammlung Albertina, Vienna

RICHARD GERSTL   69
The Sisters. 1905
Oil on canvas, 175 x 150 cm
Österreichische Galerie, Vienna

RICHARD GERSTL   70
Danube Canal. Ca. 1906
Oil on canvas, 63 x 46.8 cm
Galerie Würthle, Vienna

RICHARD GERSTL   71
Family Schoenberg. Ca. 1908
Oil on canvas
Museum moderner Kunst, Vienna

ALBIN EGGER-LIENZ   72
Luncheon. Ca. 1916
Oil on canvas, 90 x 139 cm
Galleria Nazionale d'Arte Moderna, Rome

ALBIN EGGER-LIENZ   73
The Spring (First Version). 1923
Oil on canvas, 85 x 126 cm
Collection Dr. Rudolf Leopold, Vienna

ANTON KOLIG   74
Berta Zuckerkandl. 1915
Oil on canvas, 150 x 81 cm
Historisches Museum der Stadt Wien

ANTON KOLIG   75
Sitting Man in a White Coat. 1920
Oil on canvas
C. Kolig, Villach

HERBERT BOECKL   76
Group on the Edge of the Woods. 1920
Oil on canvas
Museum moderner Kunst, Vienna

HERBERT BOECKL   77
Eberndorf Monastery. 1922
Oil on canvas
Österreichische Galerie, Vienna

HERBERT BOECKL   78
Still-Life with Peaches in front of a Red Background. 1925
Oil on canvas
Neue Galerie der Stadt Linz,
Wolfgang Gurlitt-Museum

WILHELM THÖNY   79
Moonlit Night on the Bank of the Mur in Graz. 1928
Oil on canvas
Österreichische Galerie, Vienna

ANTON FAISTAUER   80
Summer Snow. 1920
Oil on canvas
Museum Carolino Augusteum, Salzburg

ANTON FAISTAUER   81
Flower Still-Life, Horsetail in Vase on Armchair. 1924
Oil on canvas
Private collection

JOSEF DOBROWSKY   82
Flower Still-Life. Ca. 1939
Oil on canvas
Galerie Würthle, Vienna

JOSEF DOBROWSKY   83
Harvest during a Thunder Storm. 1948
Oil on canvas
Neue Galerie der Stadt Linz,
Wolfgang Gurlitt-Museum

KARL STARK   84
Sunny Fields in Late Autumn. 1957
Oil on canvas, 55 x 77 cm
Private collection

KARL STARK   85
Sunny Landscape with Red Roofs. 1961
Oil on canvas, 93 x 111 cm
Private collection

HANS PLANK 86
Woodcutter. 1980
Oil on canvas
In the artist's collection

HANS PLANK 87
Portrait of Sebastian. 1981
Oil on canvas
In the artist's collection

ALBIN EGGER-LIENZ 88
Study for an Old Man (for ''Pilgrim''). 1904
Drawing with black crayon
Graphische Sammlung Albertina, Vienna

ALBIN EGGER-LIENZ 89
Study for ''Women of War''. 1918
Charcoal drawing
Tiroler Landesmuseum Ferdinandeum, Innsbruck

ANTON KOLIG 90
Sitting Woman. Ca. 1920
Charcoal drawing
Galerie Würthle, Vienna

HERBERT BOECKL 91
Study of Trees on the Wörthersee
Charcoal drawing
Graphische Sammlung Albertina, Vienna

HERBERT BOECKL 92
Child's Head
Charcoal drawing
Graphische Sammlung Albertina, Vienna

HERBERT BOECKL 93
Woman Sewing (Wife of the Artist)
Charcoal drawing
Graphische Sammlung Albertina, Vienna

ALOIS WACH 94
Mother. 1919
Woodcut

WILHELM THÖNY   95
Park. 1922
Pencil drawing
Graphische Sammlung Albertina, Vienna

RUDOLF WACKER   96
Romanian Woman, Sitting. 1924
Blue pencil drawing
From R. Wacker-Sandner:
Zeichnung als Befreiung

OTTO JUNGWIRTH   97
Magda. Ca. 1974
Pencil drawing
In the artist's collection

HERBERT FLADERER   98
Mother with Child. 1952
Woodcut

HERBERT FLADERER   99
Fear. 1972
Woodcut

HANS PLANK   100
Lonely Man. 1971
Woodcut, 58 x 34.5 cm